CHRISTIAN CHART HITS

14 TOP CHRISTIAN SINGLES

ISBN 978-1-70515-610-0

7777 W. BLUEMOUND RD. P.O. BOX 13819 MILWAUKEE, WI 53213

Visit Hal Leonard Online at
www.halleonard.com

Contact us:
Hal Leonard
7777 West Bluemound Road
Milwaukee, WI 53213
Email: info@halleonard.com

In Europe, contact:
Hal Leonard Europe Limited
42 Wigmore Street
Marylebone, London, W1U 2RN
Email: info@halleonardeurope.com

In Australia, contact:
Hal Leonard Australia Pty. Ltd.
4 Lentara Court
Cheltenham, Victoria, 3192 Australia
Email: info@halleonard.com.au

BELIEVE FOR IT

Words and Music by DWAN HILL,
KYLE LEE, CECE WINANS
and MITCH WONG

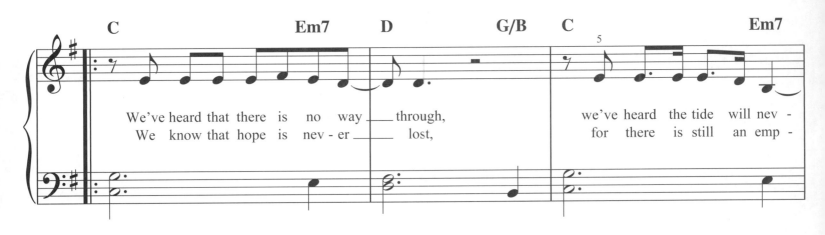

We've heard that there is no way ___ through,
We know that hope is nev-er ___ lost,

we've heard the tide will nev-
for there is still an emp-

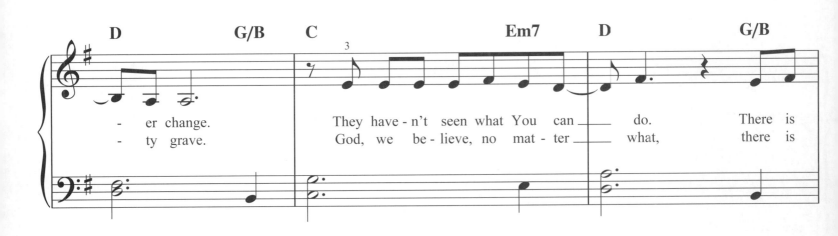

- er change.
- ty grave.

They have-n't seen what You can ___ do.
God, we be-lieve, no mat-ter ___ what,

There is
there is

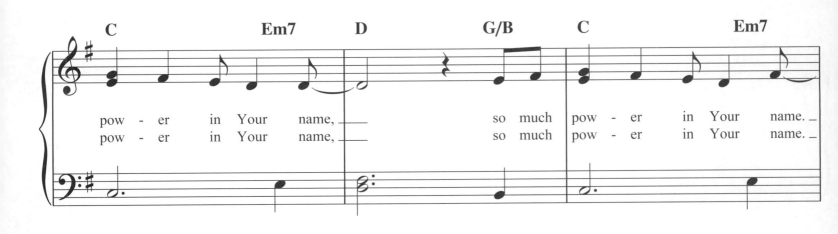

pow - er in Your name, ___
pow - er in Your name, ___

so much pow - er in Your name. ___
so much pow - er in Your name. ___

Move the im-mov-a-ble, break the un-break-a-ble.

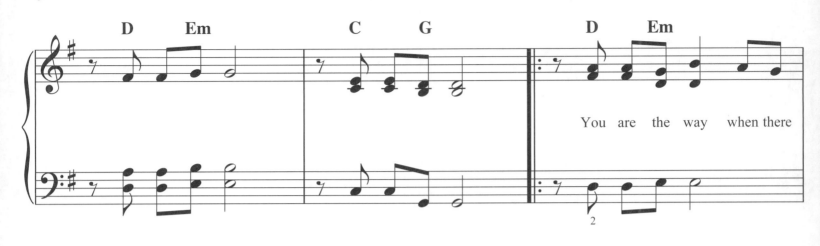

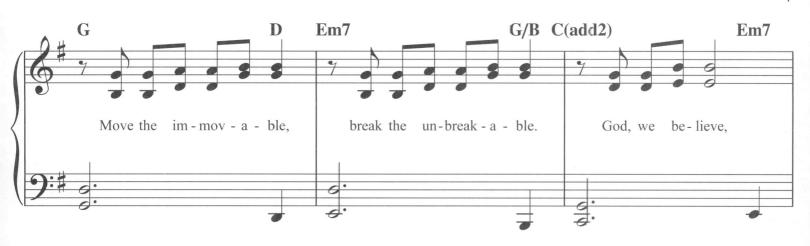

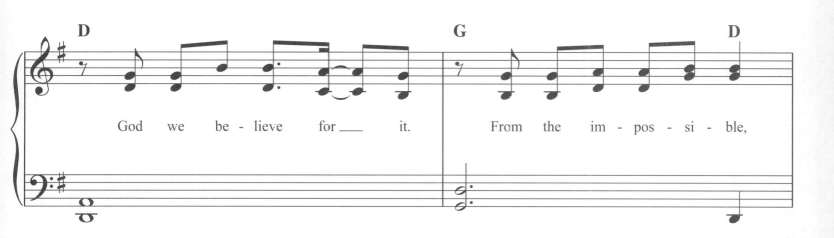

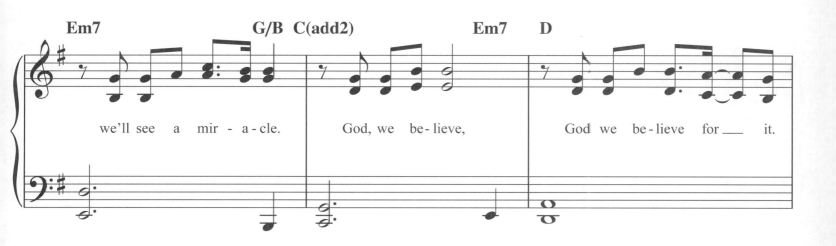

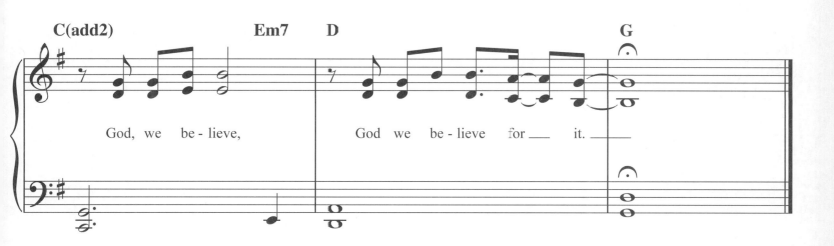

BATTLE BELONGS

Words and Music by PHIL WICKHAM
and BRIAN JOHNSON

Moderate Rock feel

When all I see is the bat-

-tle, You see my vic - t'ry. _____

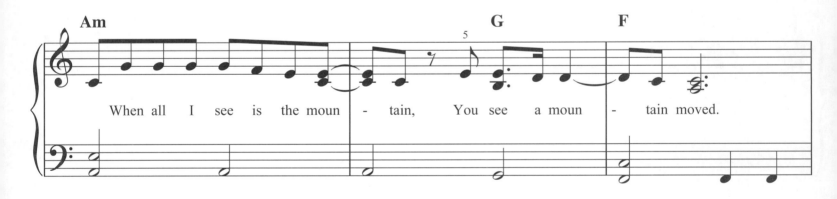

When all I see is the moun - tain, You see a moun - tain moved.

And as I walk through the shad - ow, Your love sur - rounds ____ me. ____

There's noth-ing to fear ___ now, for I am safe ___

___ with You. So, when I fight, I'll fight on my knees ___

___ with my hands lift-ed high. ___ Oh God, the bat-tle be - longs to ___ You. And ev-'ry

fear I lay at Your feet. ___ I'll sing through the night. ___ Oh God, the bat-tle be -

longs to ___ You. _____ And if You are for _

___ me, who can be a - gainst ___ me? Yeah. _____

For, Je - sus, there's noth - ing im - pos - si - ble ___ for You.

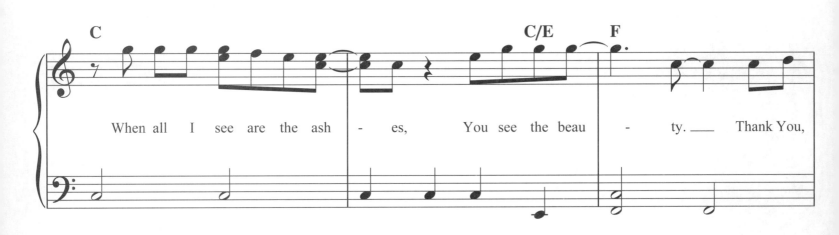

When all I see are the ash - es, You see the beau - ty. __ Thank You,

God! When all I see is the cross, ___ God, You see the emp -

- ty tomb. ___ So, when I fight, I'll fight on my knees

___ with my hands lift - ed high. ___ Oh God, the bat - tle be - longs to ___ You. And ev - 'ry

fear I lay at Your feet. ___ I'll sing through the night. ___ Oh God, the bat - tle be -

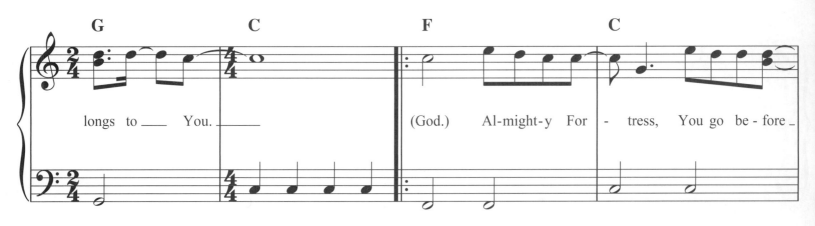

longs to ___ You. ___ (God.) Al-might-y For - tress, You go be - fore ___

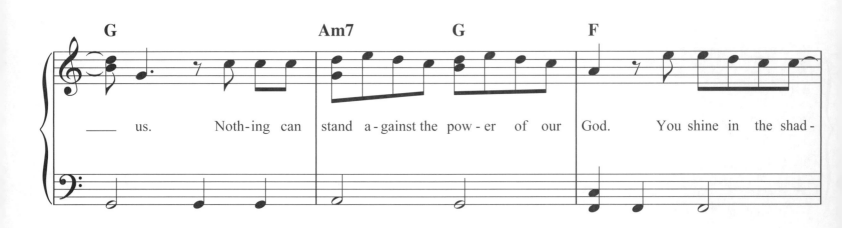

___ us. Noth-ing can stand a-gainst the pow-er of our God. You shine in the shad-

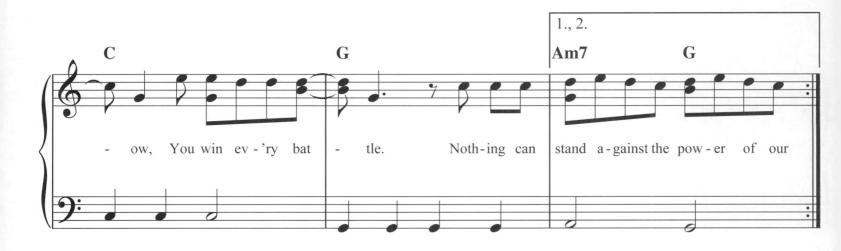

- ow, You win ev-'ry bat - tle. Noth-ing can stand a-gainst the pow-er of our

stand a-gainst the pow-er of our God. ___ So, when I

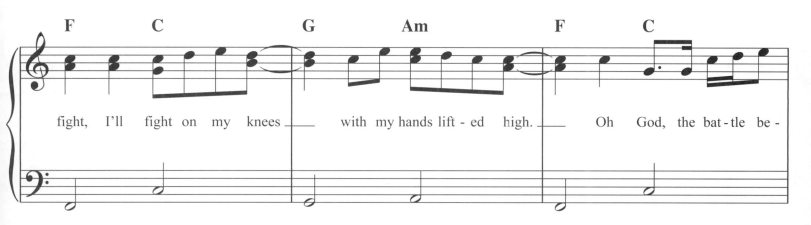

fight, I'll fight on my knees ___ with my hands lift - ed high. ___ Oh God, the bat - tle be -

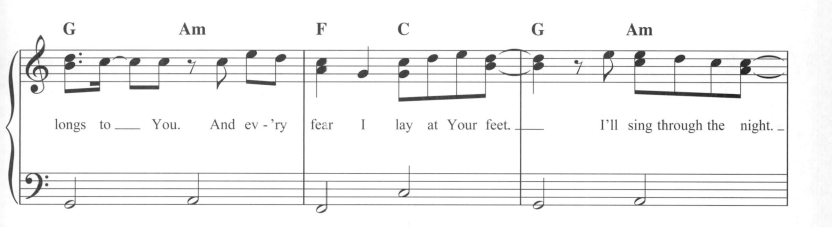

longs to ___ You. And ev - 'ry fear I lay at Your feet. ___ I'll sing through the night. ___

___ Oh God, the bat - tle be - longs to ___ You. ___ Oh God, the bat - tle be -

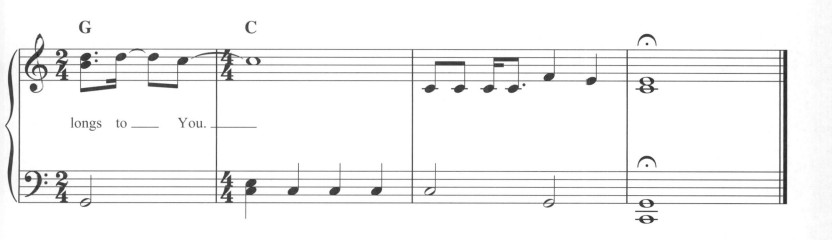

longs to ___ You. ___

THE BLESSING

Words and Music by KARI JOBE CARNES,
CODY CARNES, STEVEN FURTICK
and CHRIS BROWN

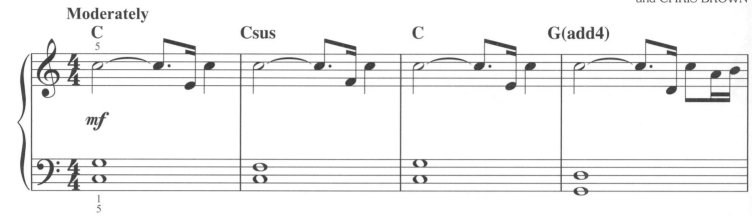

The Lord bless you ___ and keep you, make His face shine up-on ___

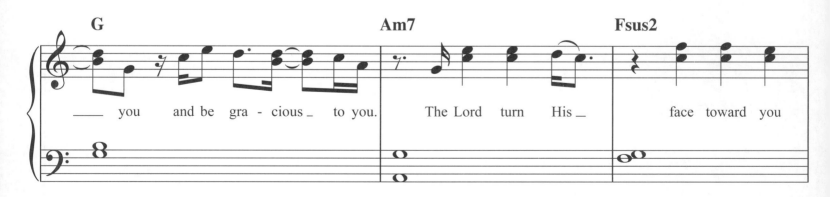

___ you and be gra-cious ___ to you. The Lord turn His ___ face toward you

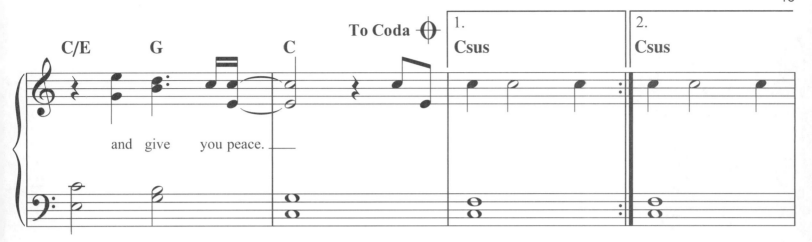

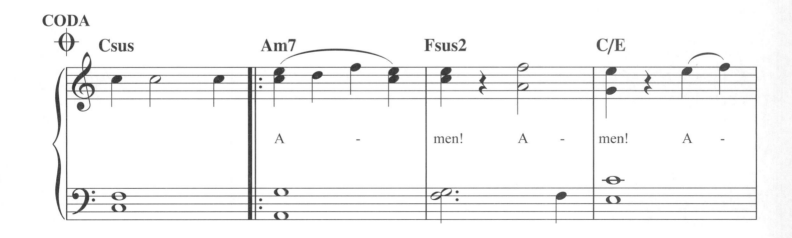

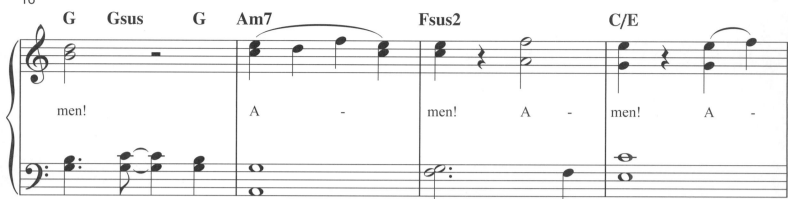

G **Gsus** **G** **Am7** **Fsus2** **C/E**

men! A - men! A - men! A -

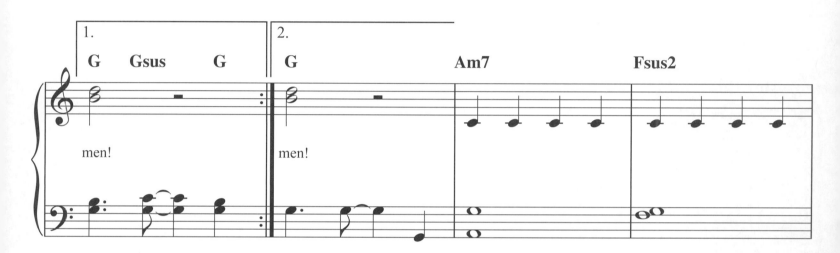

1. **G** **Gsus** **G** **2.** **G** **Am7** **Fsus2**

men! men!

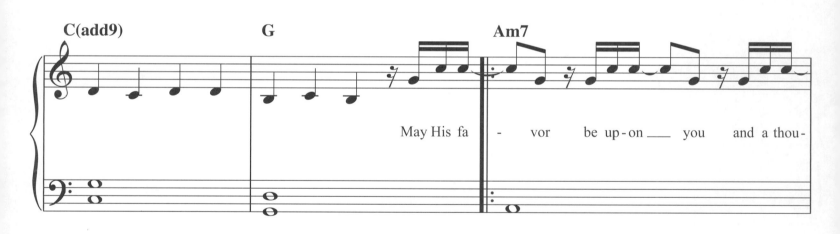

C(add9) **G** **Am7**

May His fa - vor be up-on ___ you and a thou-

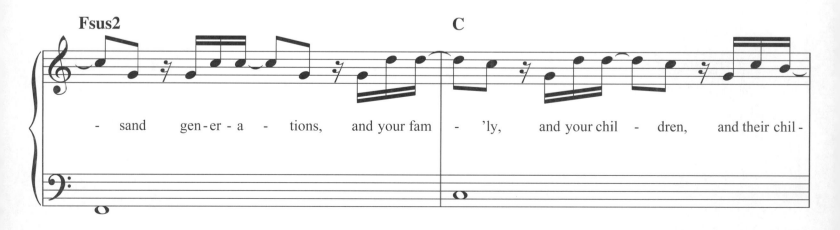

Fsus2 **C**

- sand gen-er-a - tions, and your fam - 'ly, and your chil - dren, and their chil-

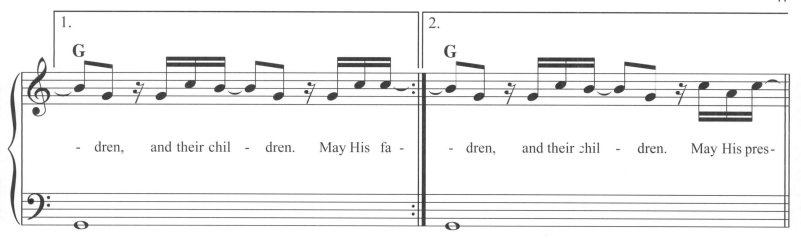

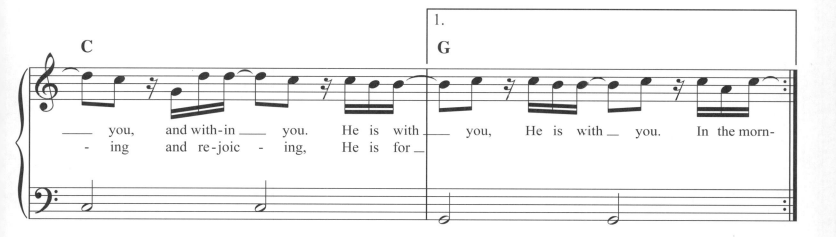

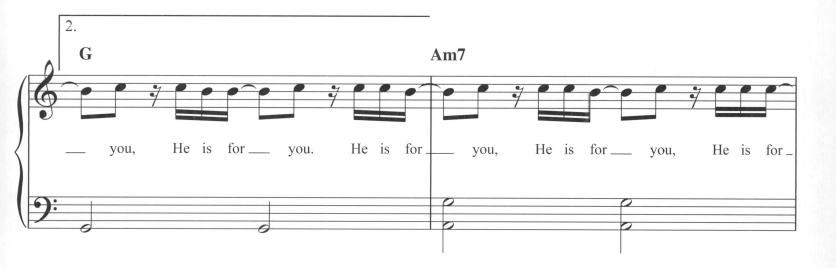

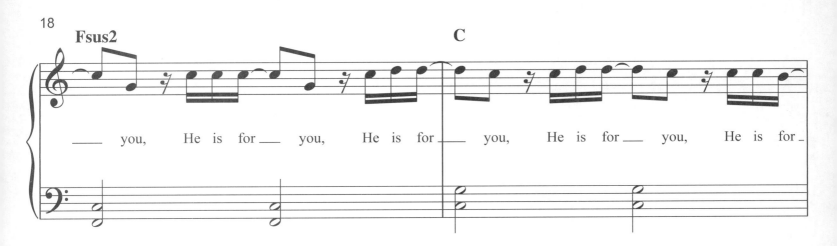

___ you, He is for __ you, He is for __ you, He is for __ you, He is for___

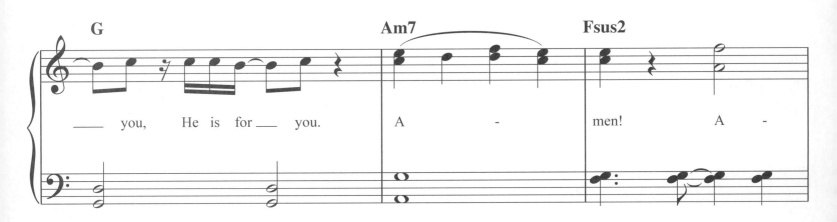

___ you, He is for __ you._ A - men! A -

men! A - men! A -

men! A - men! A - men!

HOLD ON TO ME

Words and Music by LAUREN DAIGLE,
PAUL DUNCAN and PAUL MABURY

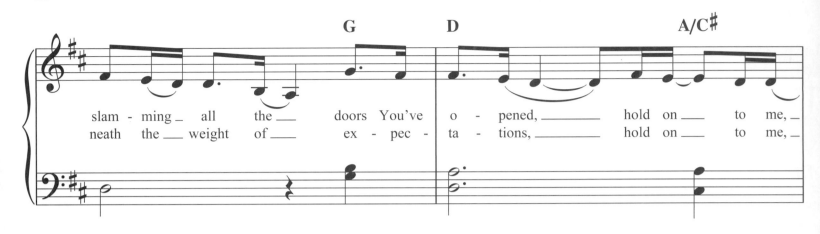

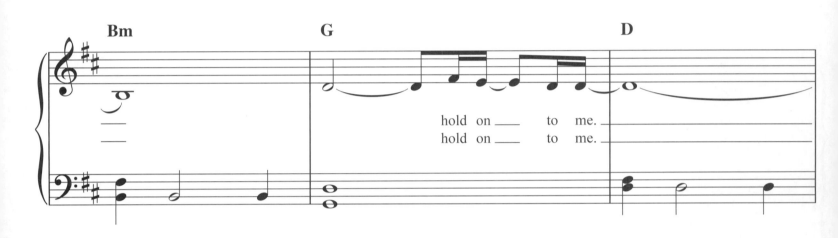

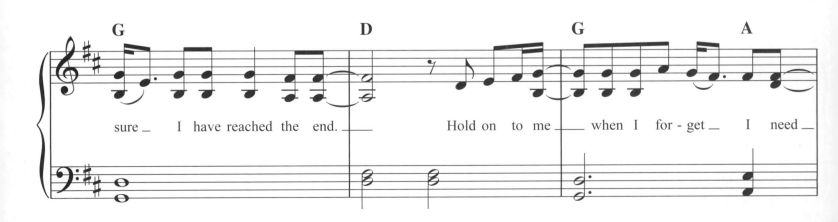

GOD ONLY KNOWS

Words and Music by JORDAN REYNOLDS,
JOEL SMALLBONE, LUKE SMALLBONE,
TEDD TJORNHOM and JOSH KERR

Moderately slow

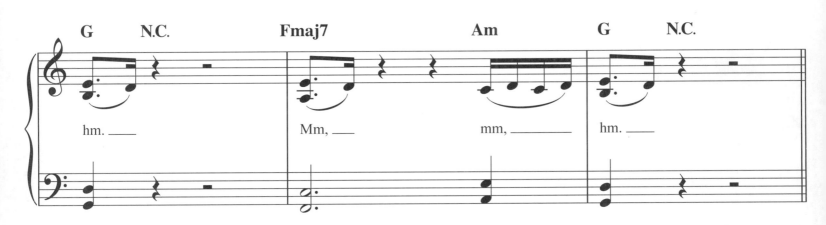

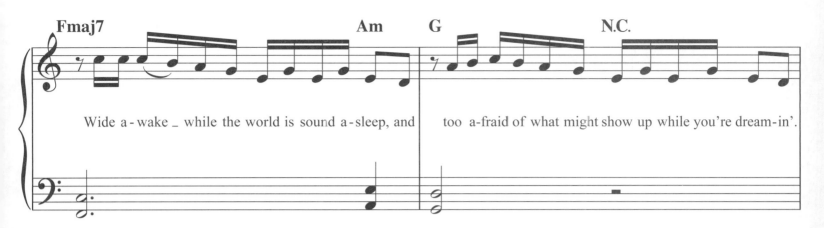

Wide a-wake _ while the world is sound a-sleep, and too a-fraid of what might show up while you're dream-in'.

No-bod-y, no-bod-y, no-bod-y sees _ you. No-bod-y, no-bod-y would be-lieve you.

Ev-'ry day you try to pick up all the piec-es. All the mem-o-ries, they some-how nev-er leave you.

No-bod-y, no-bod-y, no-bod-y sees _ you. No-bod-y, no-bod-y would be-lieve you.

(There's a kind of love that, there's a kind of love.)

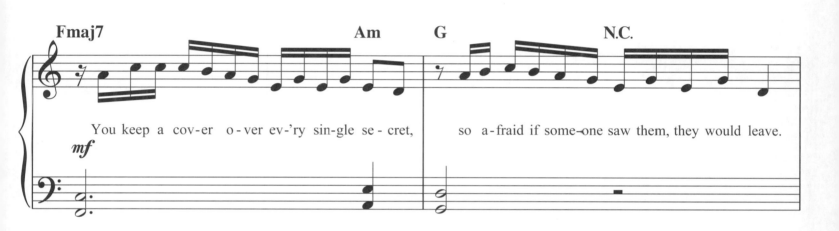

You keep a cov-er o-ver ev-'ry sin-gle se-cret, so a-fraid if some-one saw them, they would leave.

But some-bod-y, some-bod-y, some-bod-y sees __ you. Some-bod-y, some-bod-y will nev-er leave __ you.

there's a kind of love. There's a kind of love that, there's a kind of love.) For the lone-

- ly, for the a - shamed, _ the mis - un - der - stood _ and the ones to blame, _ what if we could start o -

- ver, we could start o - ver, we could start o - ver? Oh, ___ for the lone -

- ly, for the a - shamed, _ the mis - un - der - stood _ and the ones to blame, _ what if we could start o -

- ver, we could start o - ver, we could start o - ver? There's a kind of love that God on - ly knows. _

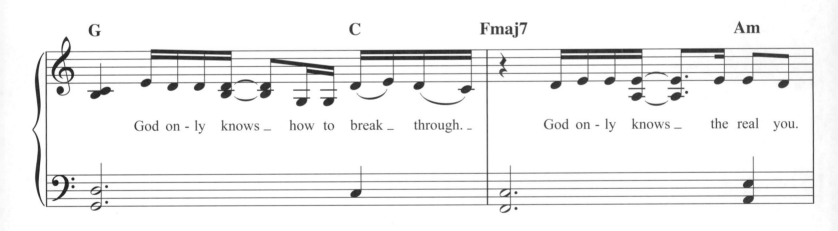

SCARS IN HEAVEN

Words and Music by MATTHEW WEST
and JOHN MARK HALL

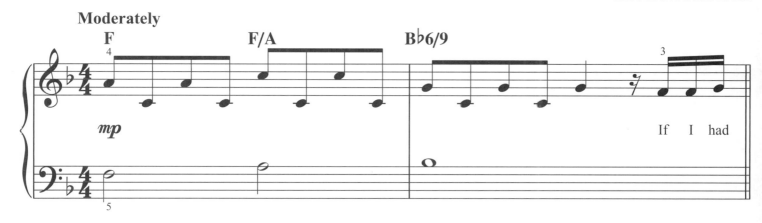

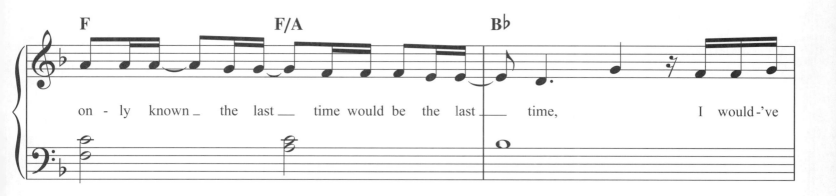

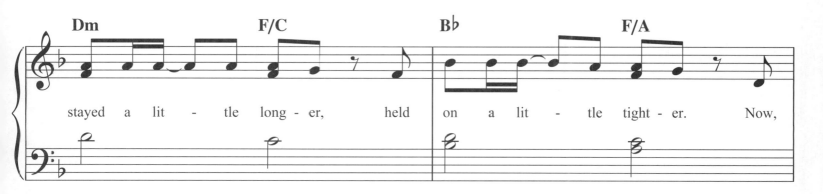

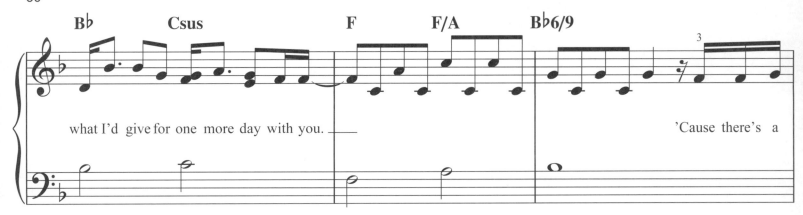

what I'd give for one more day with you. _____ 'Cause there's a

wound here in _____ my heart where some-thing's miss - ing, and they

tell me that _____ it's gon - na heal _____ with time. _____ But I

know you're in _____ a place where all your wounds have been _____ e - rased, and

know-ing yours are healed is heal-ing mine. The on-ly scars _ in heav - en, __

they won't be-long _ to me __ and you. There'll be no such thing _ as

bro-ken, ____ and all the old __ will be __ made new. And the thought that makes _ me

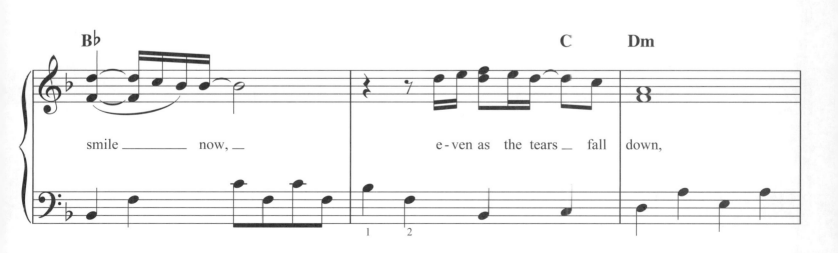

smile _____ now, _ e-ven as the tears _ fall down,

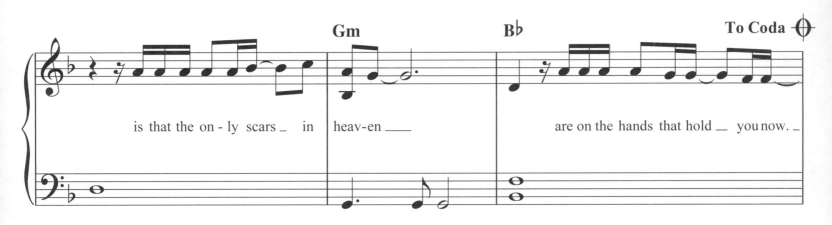

Gm   **B♭**   **To Coda** ⊕

is that the on - ly scars _ in heav-en ____ are on the hands that hold _ you now. _

F   **F/A**   **B♭6/9**   **F**   **F/A**

____ I know the road you walked _ was an - y - thing _ but eas -

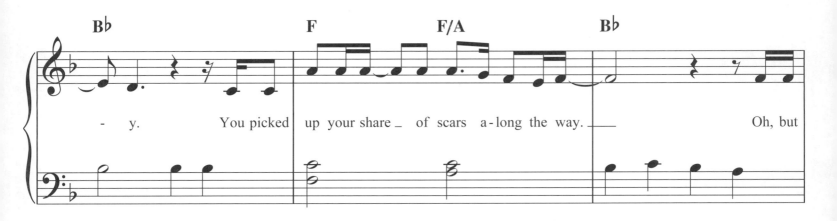

B♭   **F**   **F/A**   **B♭**

- y. You picked up your share _ of scars a - long the way. ____ Oh, but

Dm   **Csus**   **B♭**   **F/A**

now you're stand - ing in the sun, ____ you've fought your fight _ and your race _ is run. The

pain is all ___ a mil - lion miles a - way. ___ The on - ly scars ___ in

Hal - le - lu - jah! Hal - le -

lu - jah! Hal - le - lu - jah

for the hands that hold ___ you now. ___ There's not a day ___ goes by that I don't see ___

_____ you. You live on in all ____ the bet - ter parts ____ of me. Un - til I'm

stand - ing with ____ you in the sun, ____ I'll fight this fight, ____ and this race ____ I'll run, un -

til I fi - n'lly see what you can see. ____ Oh. ____

cresc.

_____ The on - ly scars ____ in heav - en, ____ they won't be - long ____ to me ____ and

_f_

you.

There'll be no such thing as bro - ken,

and all the old will be made new. And the thought that makes me smile now,

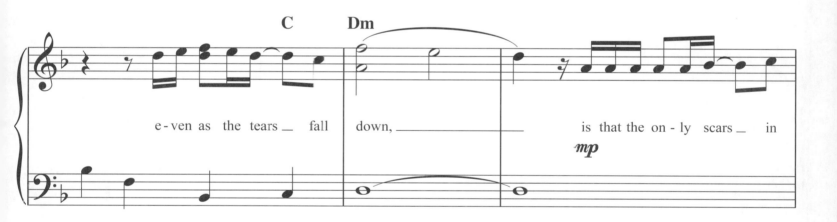

e - ven as the tears fall down, is that the on - ly scars in

heav - en are on the hands that hold you now.

GRAVES INTO GARDENS

Words and Music by CHRIS BROWN,
STEVEN FURTICK, TIFFANY HAMMER
and BRANDON LAKE

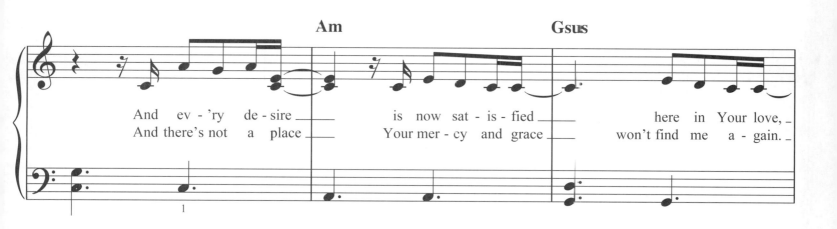

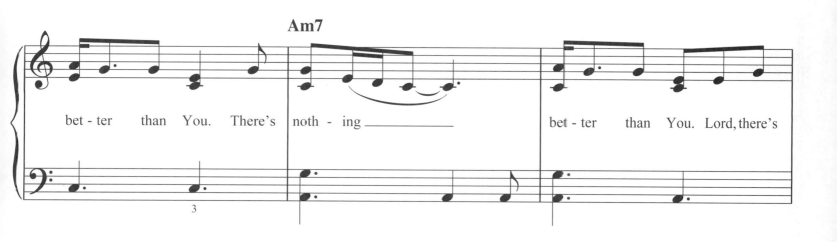

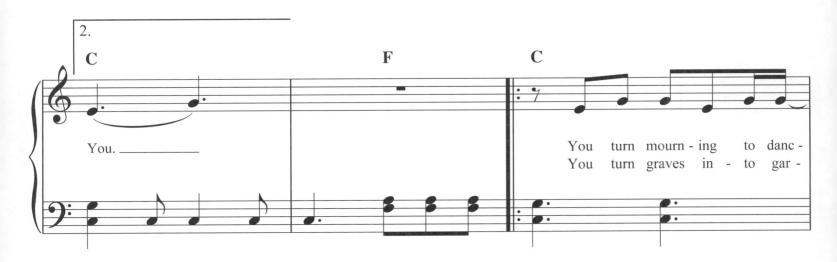

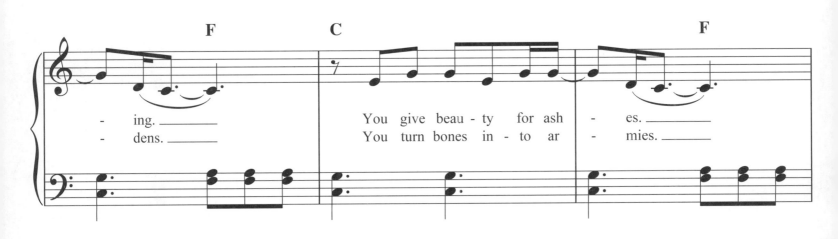

You turn shame in - to glo - ry. ____ You're the on - ly One who
You turn seas in - to high - ways. __ You're the on - ly One who

1. C

can.

2. C

can. You're the on - ly One who

C

can. Oh, there's noth - ing _____ bet - ter than You. There's

mp

Am7

noth - ing _____

bet - ter than You. Lord, there's

Fsus2

noth - ing, _____

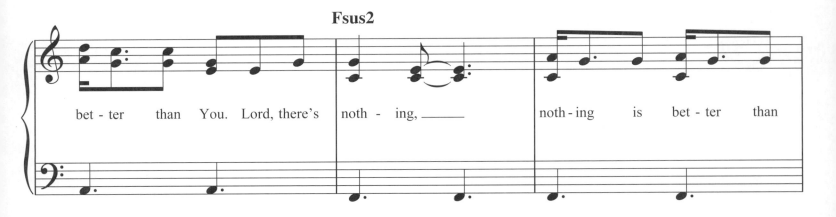

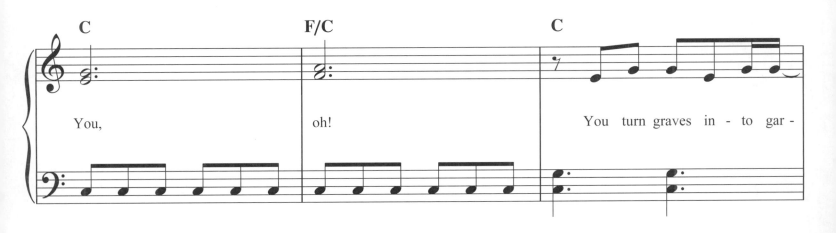

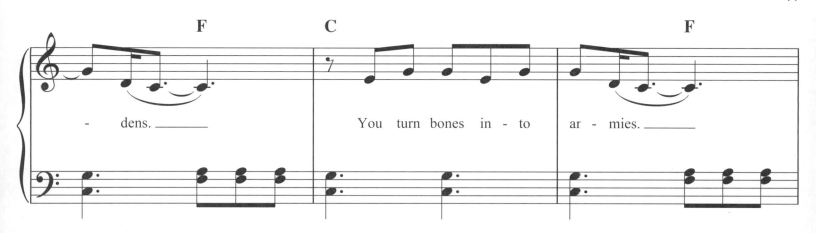

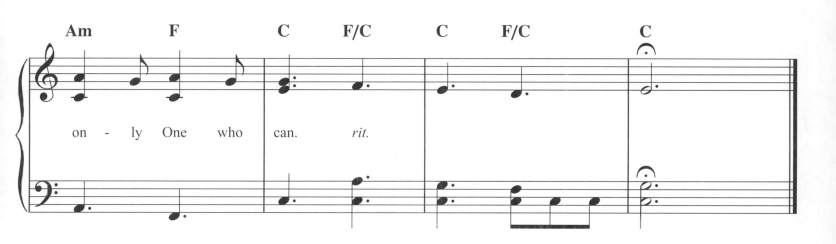

MY JESUS

Words and Music by ANNE WILSON,
JEFF PARDO and MATTHEW WEST

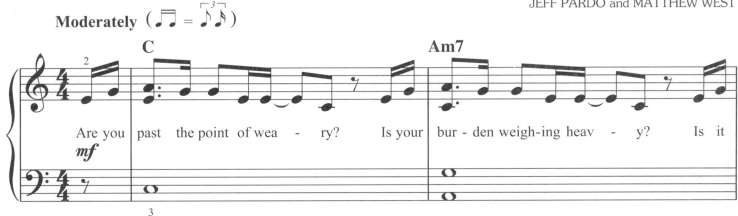

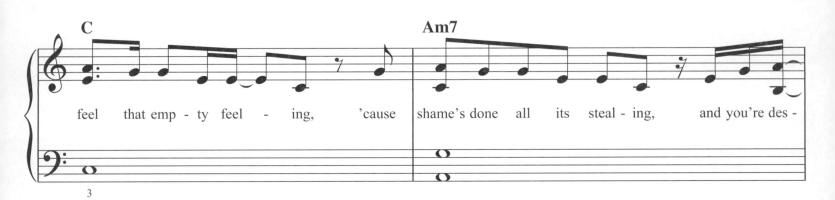

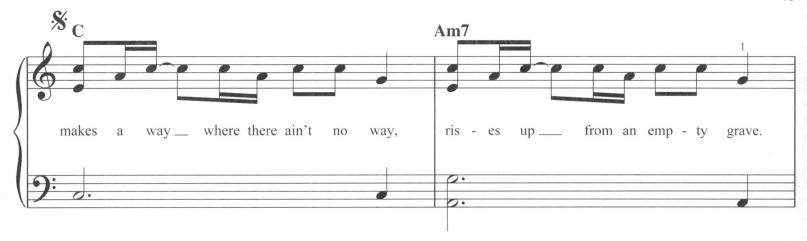

makes a way ___ where there ain't no way, ris - es up ___ from an emp - ty grave.

Ain't no sin - ner that He ___ can't save. Let me tell you 'bout my Je - sus. His

love is strong ___ and His grace is free, and the good news is, I know that He ___ can

do for you ___ what He's done for me. ___ Let me tell you 'bout my Je - sus, and

let my Je - sus change your life. ___ Hal - le - lu - jah! ___ Hal - le - lu - jah! ___

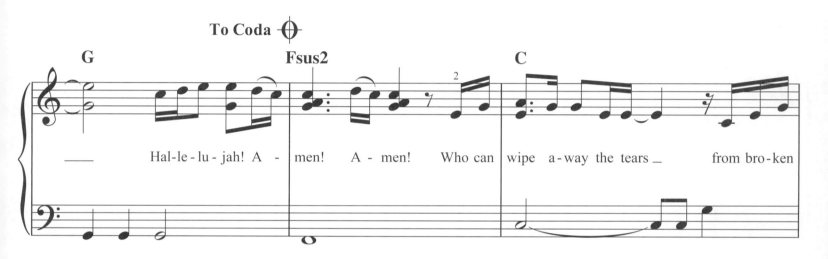

To Coda

___ Hal - le - lu - jah! A - men! A - men! Who can wipe a - way the tears ___ from bro - ken

dreams and wast - ed years, ___ and tell the past to dis - ap - pear? ___ Oh,

let me tell you 'bout my Je - sus. And all the wrong turns that you would go and

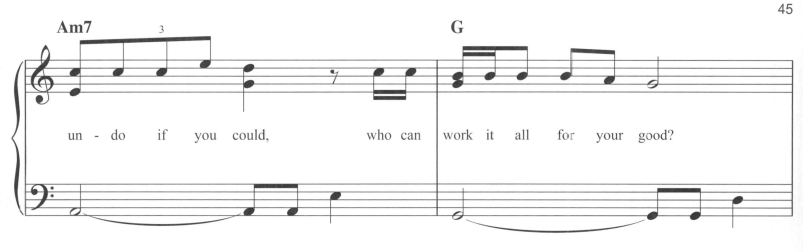

un - do if you could, who can work it all for your good?

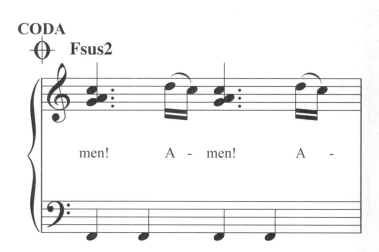

Let me tell you 'bout my Je - sus. He

CODA

men! A - men! A -

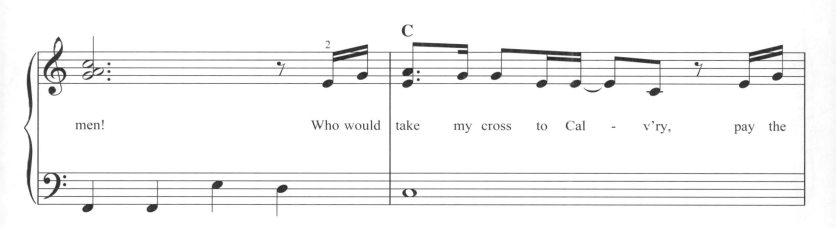

men! Who would take my cross to Cal - v'ry, pay the

price for all my guilt - y? Who would care that much a - bout __ me?

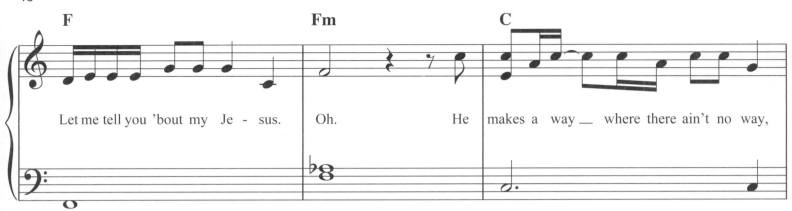

Fsus2

Let me tell you 'bout my Je - sus, and let my Je - sus change your life.

C   **Am7**   **G**

___ Hal - le - lu - jah! ___ Hal - le - lu - jah! ___ Hal - le - lu - jah! A -

Fsus2   **C**   **Am7**

men!   A - men!   Hal - le - lu - jah! ___ Hal - le - lu - jah! ___

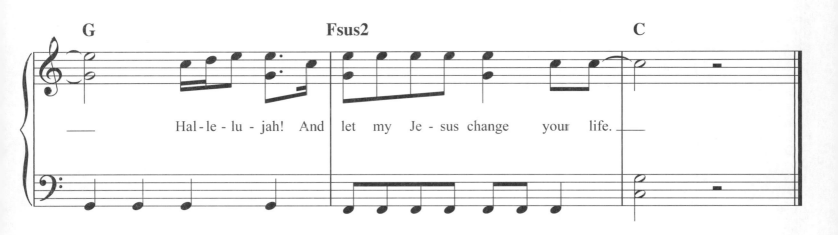

G   **Fsus2**   **C**

___ Hal - le - lu - jah! And let my Je - sus change your life. ___

RISE UP
(Lazarus)

Words and Music by MADISON CAIN,
LOGAN CAIN, TAYLOR CAIN,
ETHAN HULSE and NICK SCHWARZ

Moderately

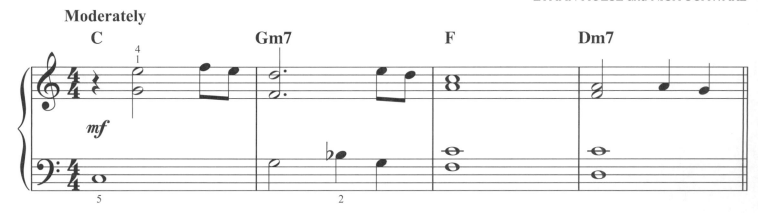

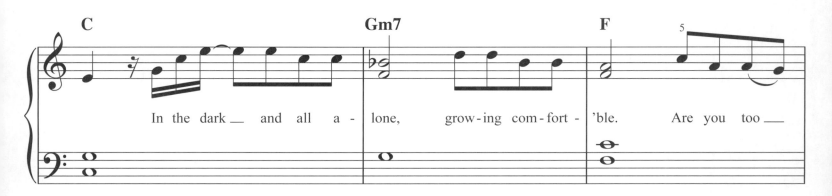

In the dark __ and all a - lone, grow-ing com-fort - 'ble. Are you too __

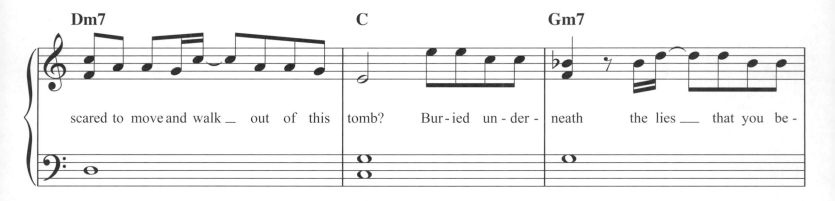

scared to move and walk __ out of this tomb? Bur-ied un-der - neath the lies __ that you be -

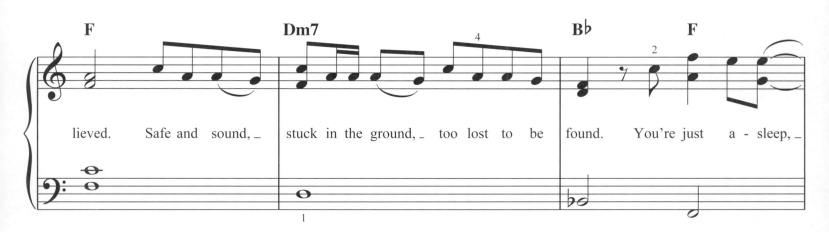

lieved. Safe and sound, __ stuck in the ground, __ too lost to be found. You're just a - sleep, __

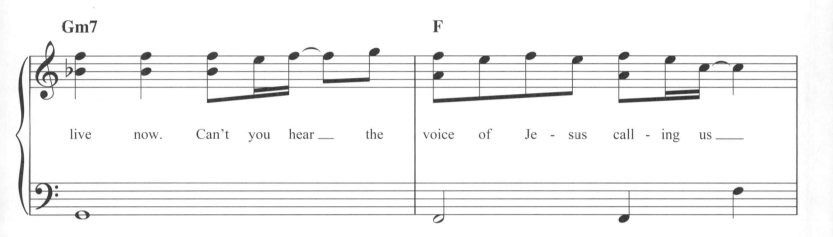

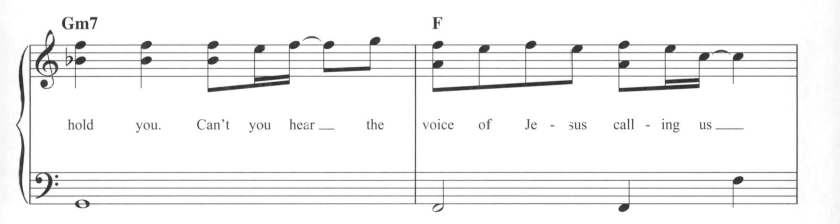

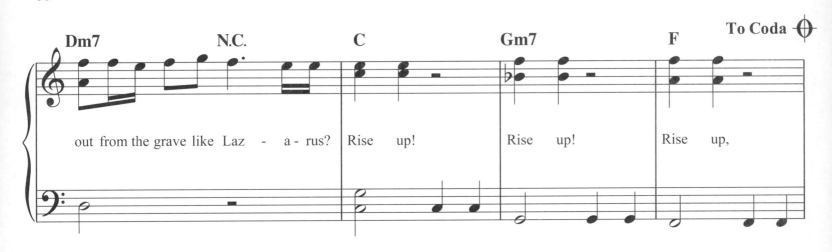

To Coda

Dm7 · N.C. · C · Gm7 · F

out from the grave like Laz - a - rus? Rise up! Rise up! Rise up,

Dm7 · C · Gm7

out from the grave like Laz - a - rus. When He said your name, the thing __ that filled your

mf

F · Dm7

veins was more __ than blood. It's the kind of love that wash - es sin __ a - way. __

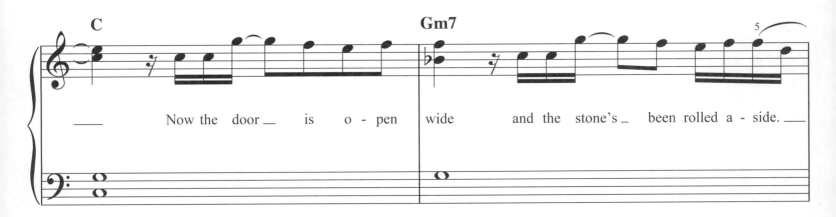

C · Gm7

__ Now the door __ is o - pen wide and the stone's __ been rolled a - side. __

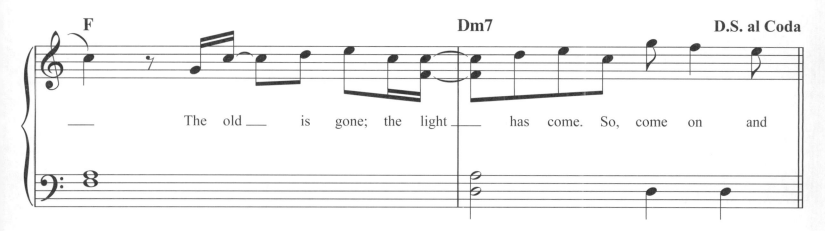

The old ___ is gone; the light ___ has come. So, come on and

out from the grave like Laz - a - rus. He's call - ing us ___ to walk out of ___ the dark. ___

___ He's giv - ing us ___ new res - ur - rect - ed hearts, ___

___ oh. ___ He's call - ing us ___ to walk out of ___ the dark. ___

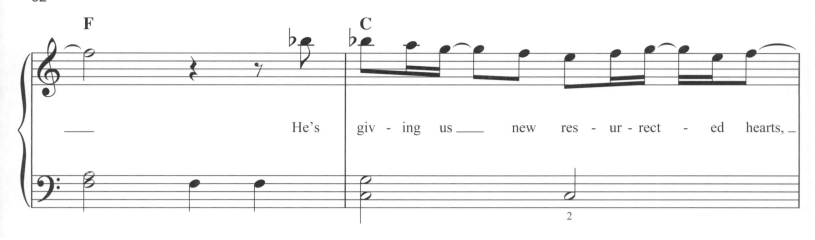

He's giv - ing us ___ new res - ur - rect - ed hearts, ___

___ oh. ___ Come on and rise up! Take a breath; ___ you're a -

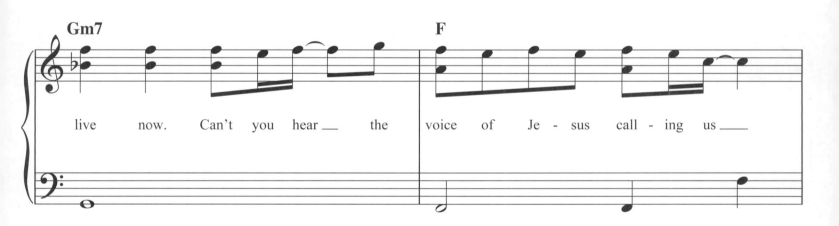

live now. Can't you hear ___ the voice of Je - sus call - ing us ___

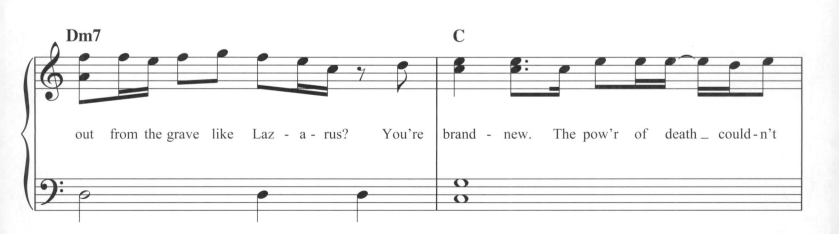

out from the grave like Laz - a - rus? You're brand - new. The pow'r of death ___ could - n't

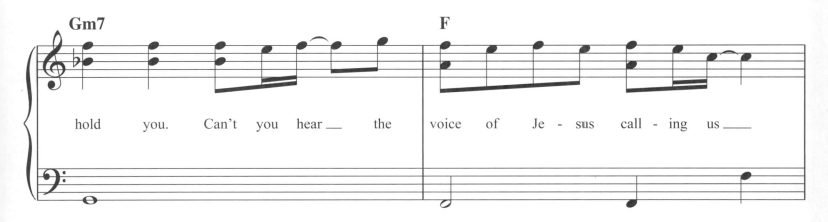

hold you. Can't you hear ___ the voice of Je - sus call - ing us ___

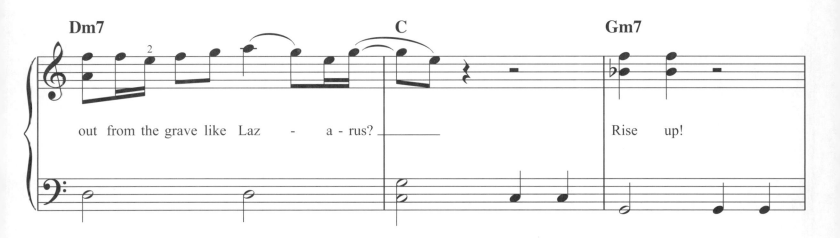

out from the grave like Laz - a - rus? ___ Rise up!

Rise up, out from the grave like Laz - a - rus. Rise up!

Rise up! Rise up, out from the grave like Laz - a - rus. ___

SEE A VICTORY

Words and Music by CHRIS BROWN,
STEVEN FURTICK, JASON INGRAM
and BEN FIELDING

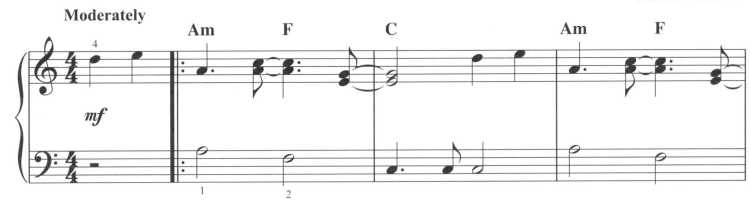

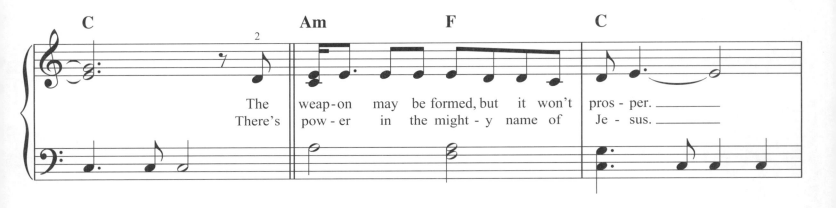

The | weap-on may be formed, but it won't | pros-per. _____
There's | pow-er in the might-y name of | Je-sus. _____

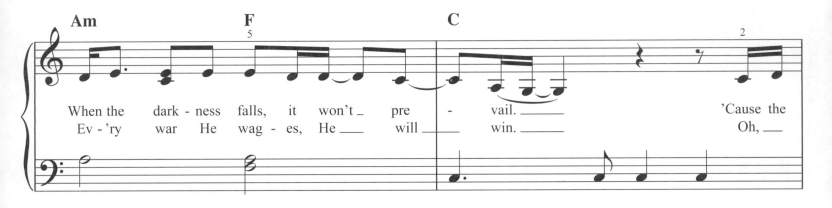

When the | dark-ness falls, it won't _ pre - | vail. _____ | 'Cause the
Ev-'ry | war He wag-es, He __ will __ | win. _____ | Oh, __

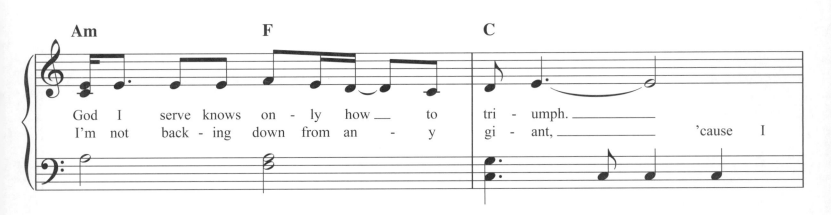

God I | serve knows on-ly how __ to | tri - umph. _____
I'm not | back-ing down from an - y | gi - ant, _____ 'cause I

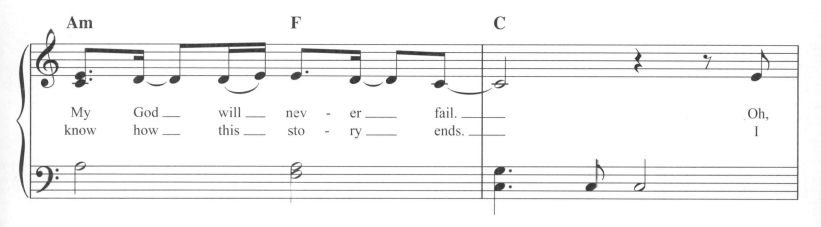

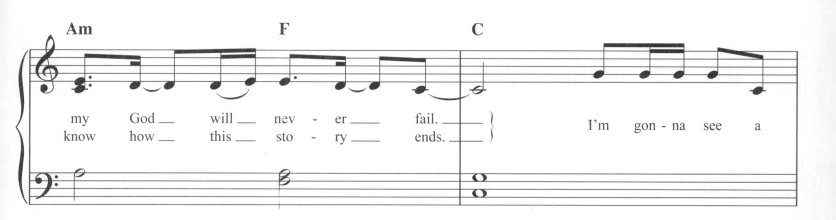

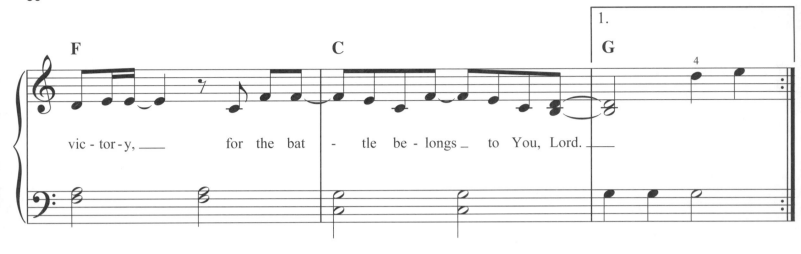

F   **C**   **1.**   **G**

vic - tor - y, _____   for the bat - tle be - longs _ to You, Lord. _____

2.   **G**   **F**   **G**   **C/E**   **F**   **Am**

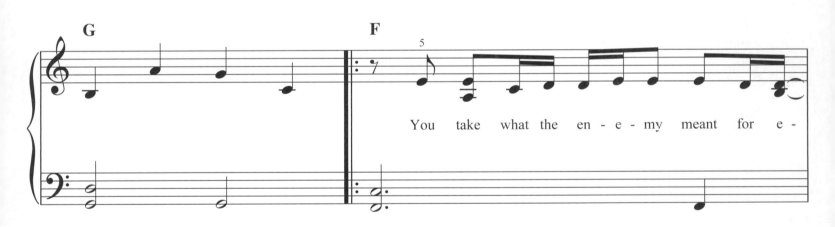

G   **F**

You take what the en - e - my meant for e -

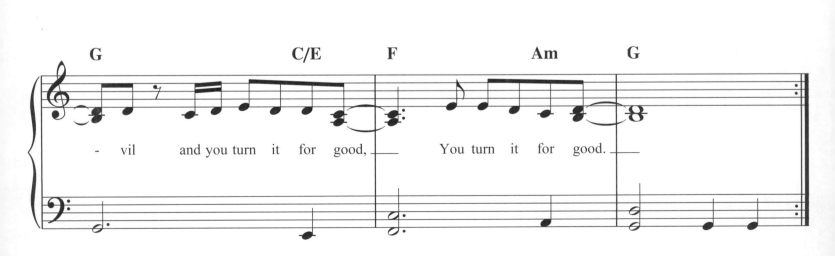

G   **C/E**   **F**   **Am**   **G**

- vil   and you turn it for good, _____ You turn it for good. _____

You take what the en - e - my meant for e - vil and You turn it for good,

You turn it for good. __ I'm gon-na see a

1.
2.

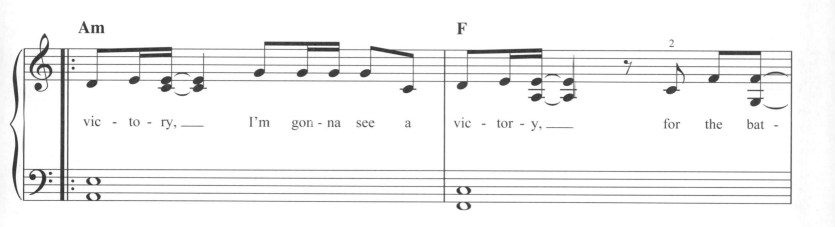

vic - to - ry, __ I'm gon-na see a vic - tor - y, __ for the bat -

- tle be - longs __ to You, Lord. __ I'm gon - na see a

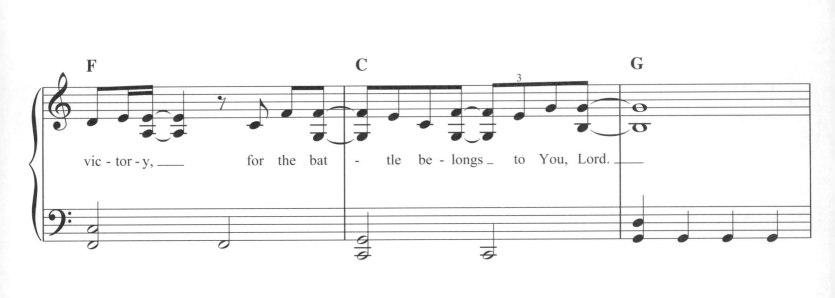

THERE WAS JESUS

Words and Music by CASEY BEATHARD,
JONATHAN SMITH and ZACH WILLIAMS

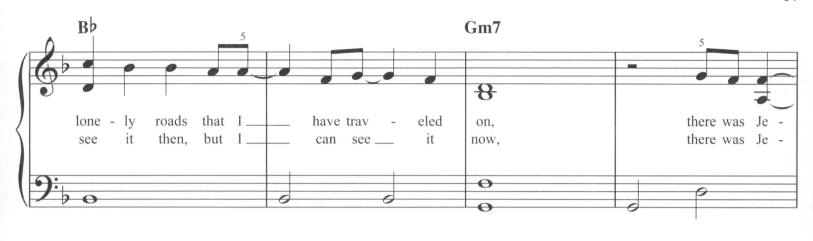

lone - ly roads that I ___ have trav - eled on,
see it then, but I ___ can see __ it now,

there was Je -
there was Je -

1.

\- sus.
\- sus.

When the

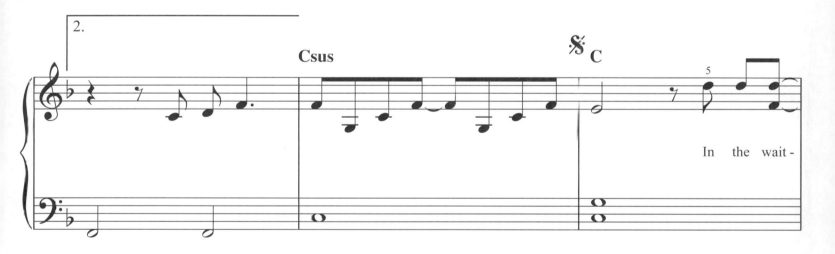

2.

In the wait -

\- ing, in the search - ing, in the heal - ing and __ the

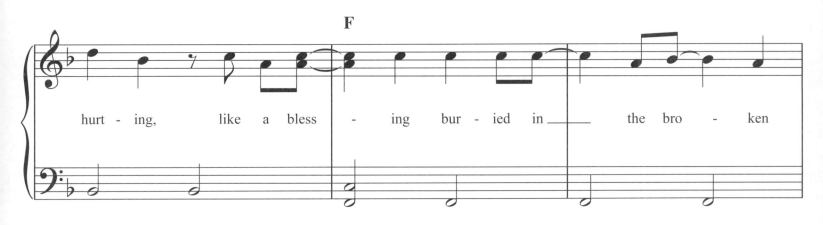

hurt - ing, like a bless - ing bur - ied in ___ the bro - ken

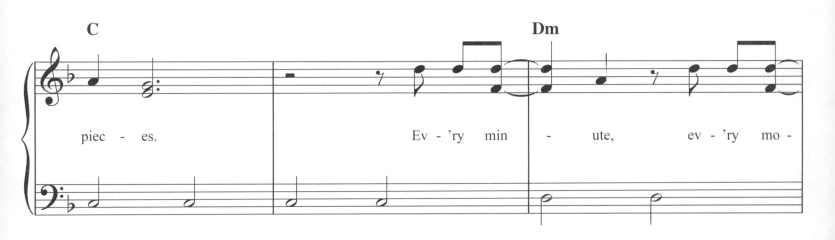

piec - es. Ev - 'ry min - ute, ev - 'ry mo -

- ment, where I've been ___ or where __ I'm go - ing, e - ven when __

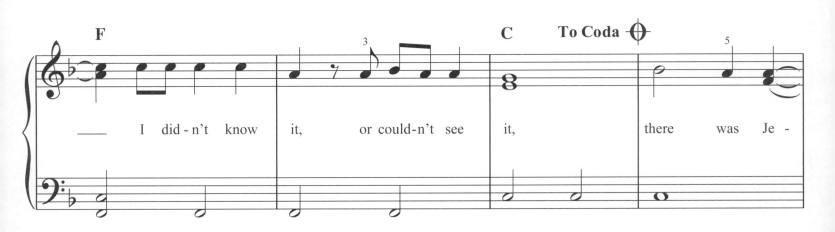

___ I did - n't know it, or could - n't see it, there was Je -

- sus.   For this man

___ who needs ___ a - maz - ing kind ___ of grace,

for for - give - ness at ___ a price ___ I could - n't pay. ___

___   I'm not per - fect, so I thank God ev - 'ry

64

day

there was Je - sus,

there was Je -

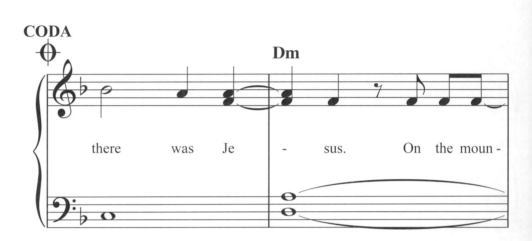

CODA

C　**D.S. al Coda**

\- sus.

Dm

there was Je - sus. On the moun -

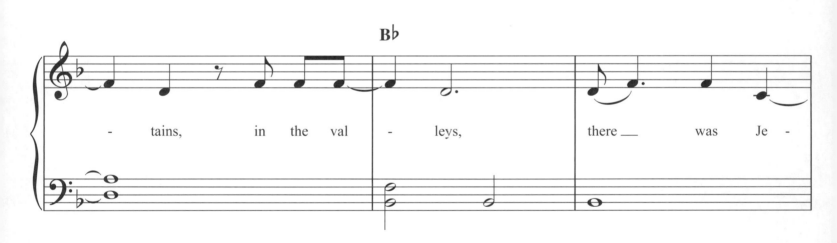

B♭

\- tains,　in the val - leys,　there ___ was Je -

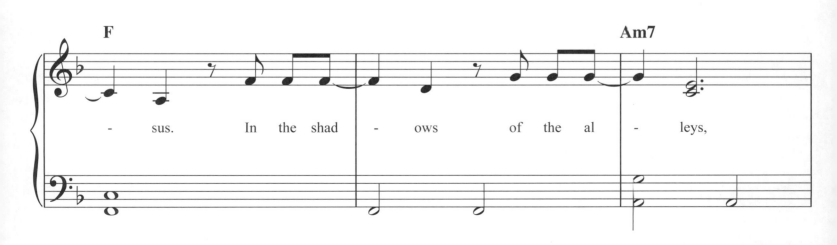

F　　　　　　　　　　　　　　　　　　**Am7**

\- sus.　In the shad - ows　of the al - leys,

there was Je - sus. In ___ the fi - re, in ___ the flood,

there ___ was Je - sus. Al - ways is and al - ways

was. ___

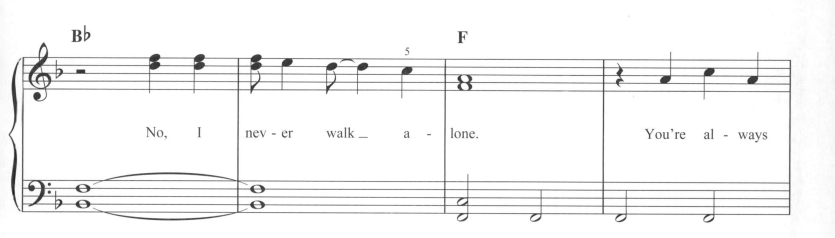

No, I nev - er walk ___ a - lone. You're al - ways

there. In the wait - ing, in the search-

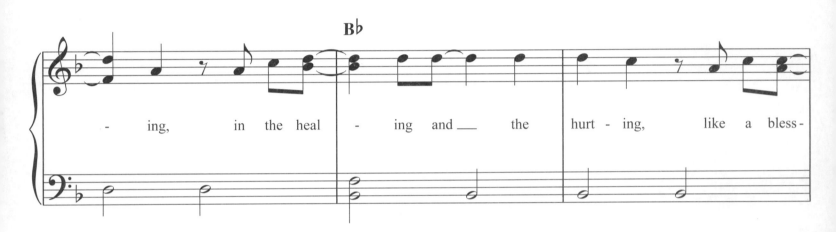

- ing, in the heal - ing and __ the hurt - ing, like a bless-

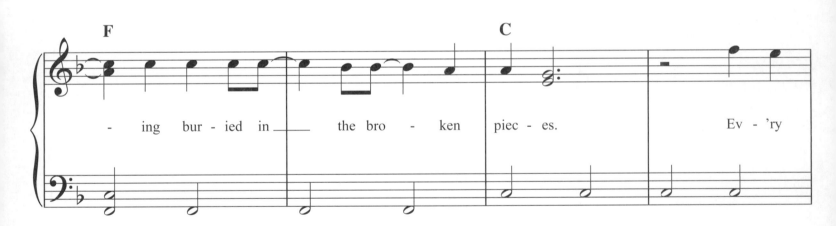

- ing bur - ied in __ the bro - ken piec - es. Ev - 'ry

min - ute, ev - 'ry mo - ment, where I've been __ or where __ I'm

go - ing, e - ven when ___ I did - n't know it, or could - n't see

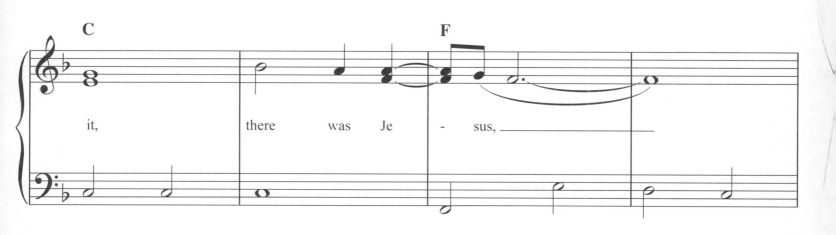

it, there was Je - sus, _____

there was Je - sus. (There was Je - sus.)

rit. There was Je - sus.

WHO YOU SAY I AM

Words and Music by REUBEN MORGAN
and BEN FIELDING

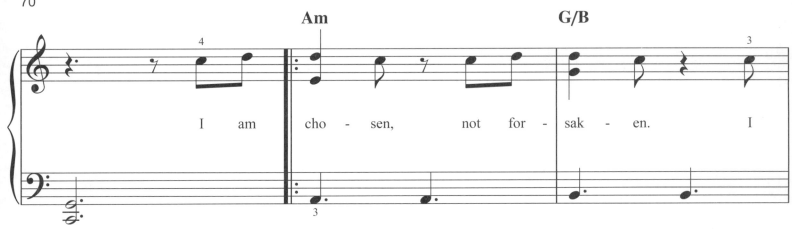

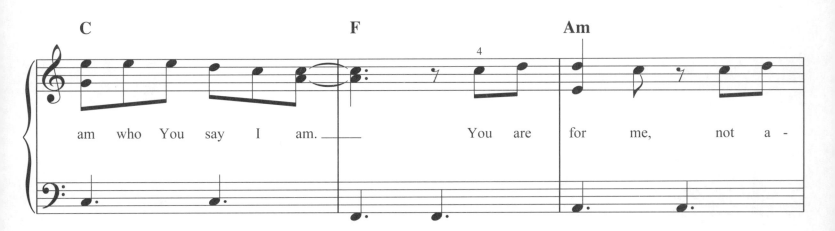

Son sets free, oh, is free in - deed.⎫
Fa - ther's house there's a place for me.⎭ I'm a

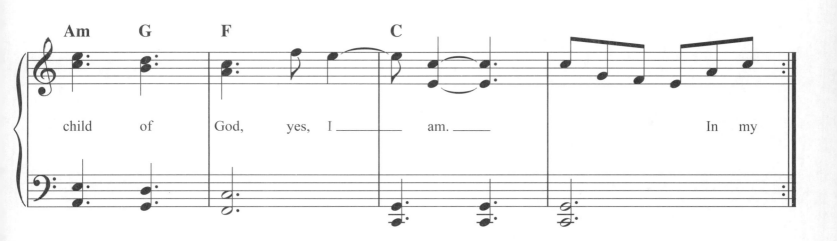

child of God, yes, I ____ am. ____ In my

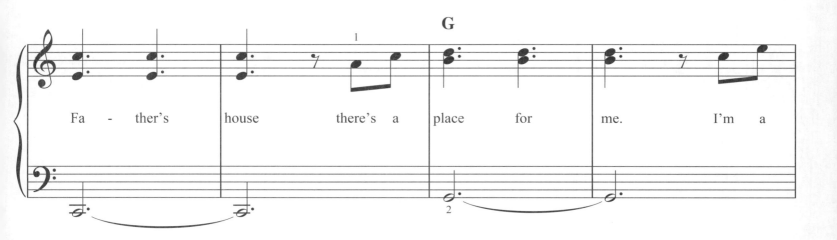

Fa - ther's house there's a place for me. I'm a

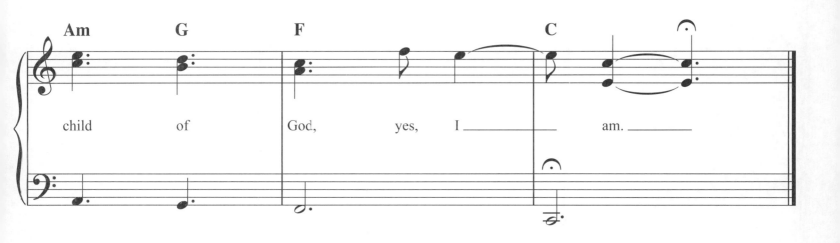

child of God, yes, I ____ am. ____

YOU SAY

Words and Music by LAUREN DAIGLE,
BEBO NORMAN, PAUL MABURY,
JASON INGRAM and MICHAEL DONEHEY

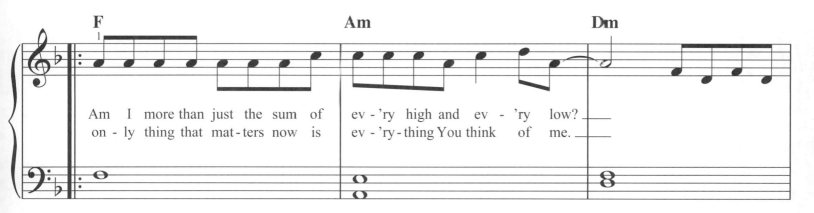

Am I more than just the sum of ev-'ry high and ev-'ry low? ___
on-ly thing that mat-ters now is ev-'ry-thing You think of me. ___

Re-mind me once a-gain just who I am, be-cause I need to know.
In You I find my worth, in You I find ___ my i-den-ti-ty.

Ooh, oh. You say I am loved when I can't feel a

mf

thing. You say I am strong when I think I am weak. And You say I am

held when I am fall - ing short. And when I don't be - long, oh, You say I am

Yours, and I be - lieve, oh, I be - lieve what You say of me. I be -

1. lieve. The
2. lieve.
Tak-ing all I have, and now I'm

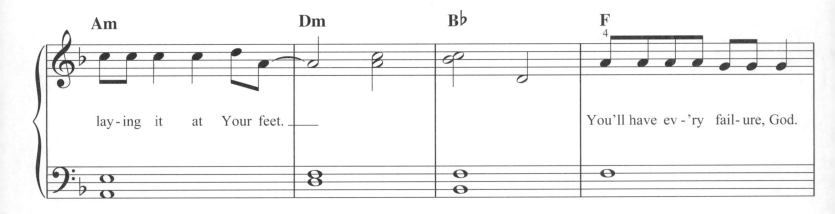

lay-ing it at Your feet. You'll have ev - 'ry fail - ure, God.

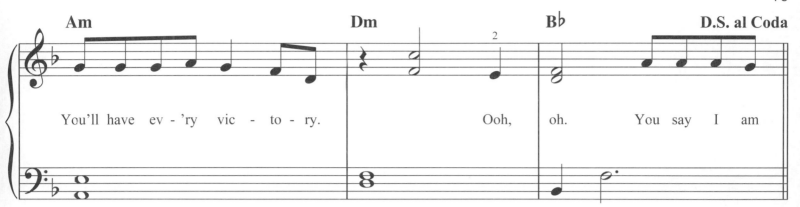

You'll have ev-'ry vic-to-ry.   Ooh,   oh.   You say   I   am

lieve.   Oh,   I   be - lieve.   Yes,   I   be - lieve   what   You   say   of

me.   I   be - lieve.

HOLY WATER

Words and Music by ED CASH,
SCOTT CASH, MARTIN CASH,
FRANNI CASH and ANDREW BERGTHOLD

God, I'm on ___ my knees ___ a-gain. ___ God, I'm beg-ging "please" ___ a-gain. ___ I need You, oh, I

need You. Walk-ing down ___ these des - ert roads, ___ wa-ter for ___ my thirst - y soul. ___ I

need You, oh, I need You. Your for - give-ness is like sweet, sweet hon-ey on my ___

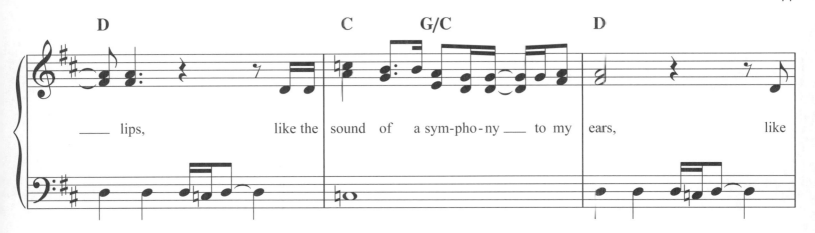

_____ lips, like the sound of a sym-pho-ny _____ to my ears, like

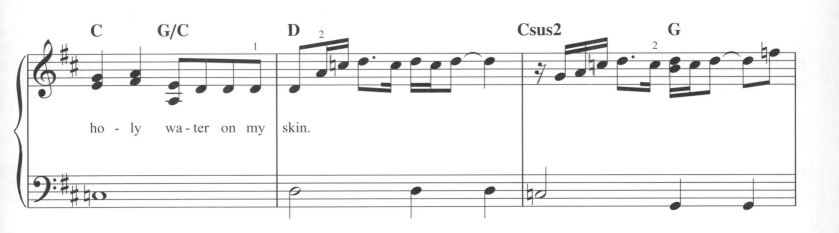

ho - ly wa-ter on my skin.

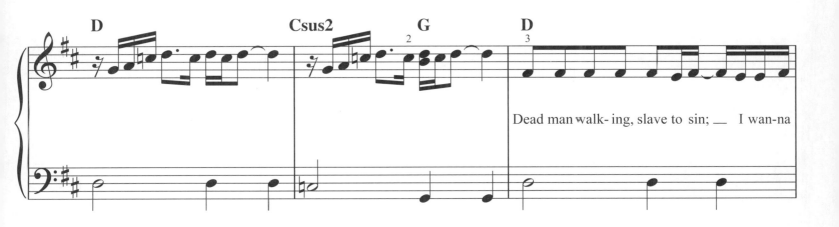

Dead man walk-ing, slave to sin; ___ I wan-na

know a-bout be - ing born ___ a - gain. ___ I need You, oh, God, I need You. So,

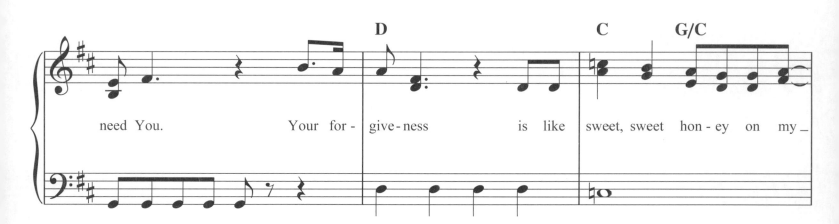

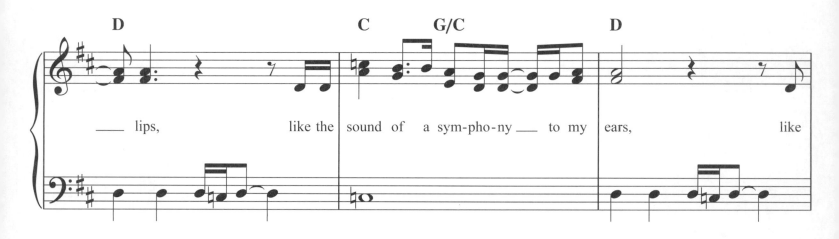

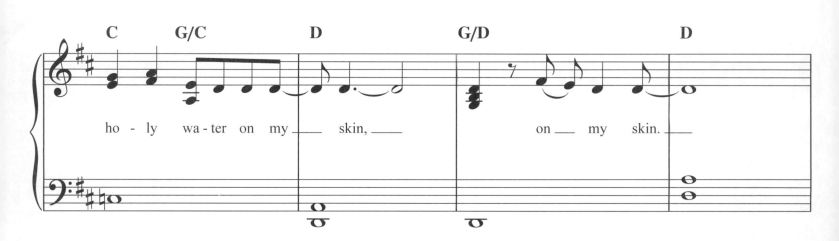

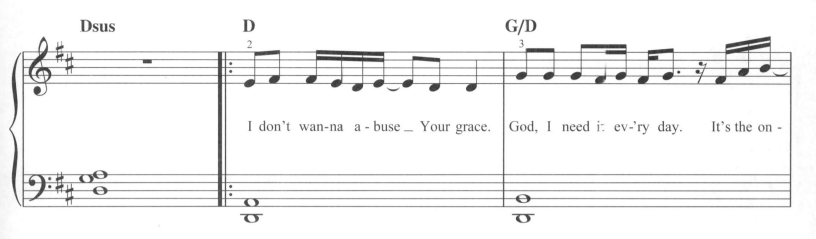

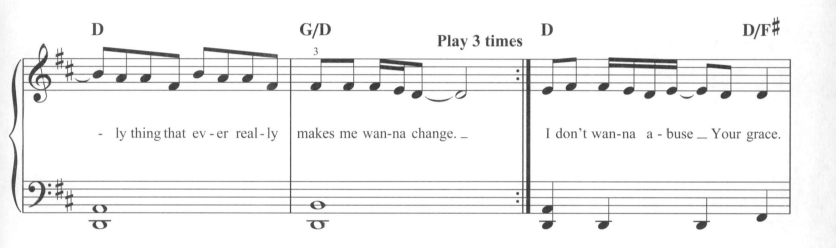

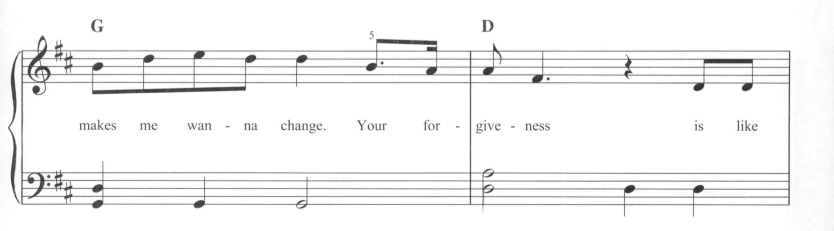

sweet, sweet hon - ey on my ___ lips, like the sound of a sym-pho-ny ___ to my

ears, like ho - ly wa-ter on my ___ skin. It's like ho - ly wa-ter on my ___

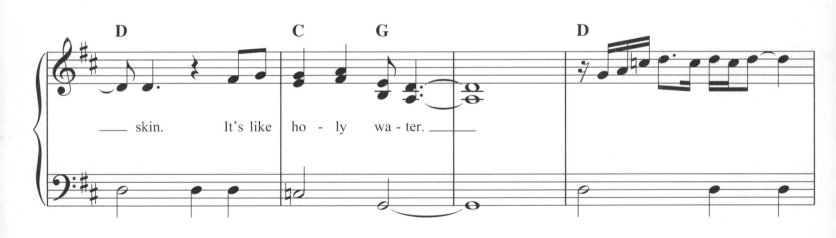

___ skin. It's like ho - ly wa - ter. ___

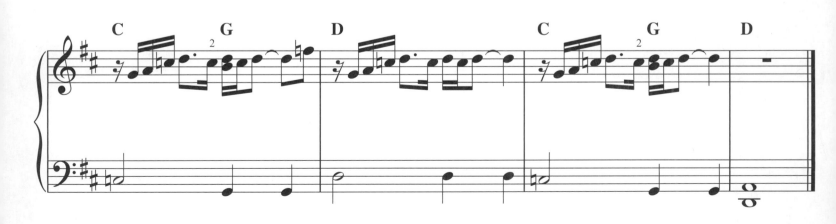